Network-KING

Your Powerful
To The Point Publishing
Book

Network-KING
*Biblical Principles on How
and Why to Build Your
Network*

Tere Kampe

Tere Kampe

Published by **To The Point Publishing**
Next Stage Communications
A Subsidiary of Next Stage Speaking

Next Stage Communications
3011 Rigell
Las Vegas, NV 89102

ISBN: 978-1-7338602-9-1

Network-KING

Table of Contents

Contents

Tere Kampe

Acknowledgments

First and foremost, I give thanks to my Lord and Savior, Jesus Christ. I came to a saving faith as a young teenager. However, you would have never known that until I was nearly 30 years old. God gave me time to get a relationship with Him figured out. I am thankful for that grace.

I am hopeful that this book is pleasing to my parents, Mike & Betty Kampe. It was their example that taught me what persistence, tenacity, integrity, commitment, loyalty, humility, and personal growth truly looks like. I mean, how it is really, lived out. Not just words used to make someone look and sound good from stage.

To my team members. Those who are simply members and those who are passionately pursuing their own dreams and goals. For everyone who came in and stayed or left. I have learned and grown so much because of each of you. Thank you for blessing my life.

Lastly, I want to thank my wife, Mary Kampe. She has been my champion for decades. Always encouraging me to get on stages and speak or write. When we first met, I had little materially.

However, I did have goals! I had a desire for a better life. She told me, even then, that one day I would stand on stages all over the world and inspire others. Thank you, hon, for your never-ending belief in me.

Tere Kampe

Foreward

Having been involved in the network marketing profession myself for the last 13 years, I can speak from experience that as a believer in the Lord Jesus Christ as my one and only Savior who has the spiritual gift of evangelism, network marketing is one of the best ways I know of to meet new people from around the world and get involved in their lives.

As a Christian, the chief aim of my life is to glorify God in all that I do and say. I want to know Him and make Him known.

Today the world is more connected than ever. On a typical day, I might talk to someone who is in South Africa in the morning and another friend who is in Europe in the afternoon and connect with old friends in Australia at night. What do all these people have in common? I met them all through network marketing.

I have been given an incredible opportunity to share the Gospel with people the Lord brings across my path. In fact, one of the greatest joys of my life is when people reach out to me via Facebook messenger, email, or in-person and tell me they heard me share the Gospel message clearly and subsequently placed their faith in Jesus Christ as their only means of salvation. These people are now my joy and my crown.

Today we are living in perilous times. People are looking for answers. False teachings and false preachers are rampant. It has never been easier to have your ears tickled by men who preach what you want to hear. It has never been easier to find a "preacher" who believes in the same "god" that you made up in your mind.

I believe it is crucial in today's world to speak the truth in love. It is crucial to get the Gospel right. What is the Gospel message that is to be preached to a lost and dying world? The Gospel is, "my friend; you are a sinner. Jesus Christ died for your sins and rose again. Trust in Him alone, and He will save you eternally. Do it now!"

If you are currently involved in network marketing, you already know how many people stand on stage at a big event and thank "god" for helping them achieve a rank or income level. When someone says that I usually say out loud from the front row, "Which god?" People in network marketing are just a snapshot of the world. Most people believe that everyone goes to heaven no matter what you believe. They believe all roads lead to heaven, which is not true.

The one thing that I have learned after 13 years in network marketing and building a team of more than 250,000 people is this: most people do not know the Lord. So I enjoy meeting new people and sharing the gospel with them.

I believe that there is nothing inherently wrong with network marketing. God expects us to work and provide for our families. There is a right way to build a network marketing business. The right way to build is to rely on the Lord and walk by faith. We do the best we can do every day, and we do the things that we can do, and we let God do the things that only He can do. We get ourselves in trouble when we make our business more important than God, which is idolatry.

As we examine our own lives, are we doing the things God has required of us? Are we daily spending time in His word? Are we attending the best church we can find faithfully? Are we a cheerful giver of our money? Are we using our time to Glorify Him? Are we using His money in a manner that would please Him? Are we using our spiritual gift to build up the body of Christ? Are we daily examining ourselves to see if there is any sin in us? Are we keeping a short account with the Lord, confessing our known sins daily? Are we filled with the Spirit, or are we a carnal Christian?

When we are doing what we should be doing, then we can have peace and joy knowing that God is sovereign. Just as we were saved by faith, we walk by faith. We trust that God has a plan for our life, which includes our business life. He is the one who can make the right connections happen for us. He can make our business grow if He wants it to. We, as spirit-filled believers, look at this life as a dot at the end of a sentence. We already have eternal life. The focus of our life becomes not looking at people we met as the next potential superstar on our team, but rather as a person for whom Christ died who we can share the Gospel with if they don't know Him as their personal Savior. We can become obsessed with that person's eternal destiny and Spiritual walk with the Lord as we point him or her to Christ.

The Bible teaches that God rewards believers who are not stingy but generous. Be a generous giver. Give to ministries that have sound doctrine. Be diligent in studying God's word. Be able to spot error from truth. Love people. Show an interest in their lives. Live out the impossible Christian life the best you can right in front of them.

I have known Tere Kampe for ten years. Tere loves God and loves people. In this book, Tere lays a foundation to help the believer look at building their network marketing business from a biblical perspective. The believer in Christ would do well to learn these principles.

David Pietsch
Voted top 30 Network Marketers in the World - 2019
Multi-Million Dollar annual earner
Eric Worre's Million Dollar Hall of Fame award
Doctor of Chiropractic

Network-KING

Introduction

This book is for those of you who aspire to greater success in your life overall and within your Network Marketing Business. I believe that the two are inextricably intertwined. I have been around the Network Marketing industry for 49 years, as of this writing. My parents joined Amway when I was eight years old, 1971. I watched them grow, set goals, fail, set new goals, fail bigger, and grow more. Then, set goals again and achieve them. They went through the very difficult years of the FTC audit of Amway. In total, they invested 43 years, with some success. However, they never got to the higher ranks they had hoped for.

I swore I would never do what they did as I saw the difficult part of their business through my teenage years. At 30 years of age, I decided to give it a shot. More on that later. I worked at it for six years, giving everything I had, while working my job – to cover "today's dollars." I had very little success. VERY LITTLE! That was from 1990 to 1996.

I concluded that I was not good at such a business. So, I put my dreams on the shelf and focused on my job again – today's dollars, as I describe it—six years in, no days off – no success. What I did get was cynical, discouraged, and almost divorced after that endeavor. Fortunately, God had His sovereign hand on all of it. I just did not realize it at the time.

Mary, my wife, and I spent seven years after that being bitter, resentful, etc. Proverbs 13:12 says, *"Hope deferred makes the heart sick."* Our hearts were really sick. We had seen a life that we desired and didn't come close to attaining it! We had big marital problems for many reasons after that. However, through that time, in roughly 2004, God began to get a hold of my heart in a big way. I began serving at our church in various ways for several years. That culminated in my becoming an elder at that church for six years – 2008 to 2014. And later, in 2016, I actually began to pastor a church in San Jose, CA.

In November of 2009, I was approached by our former pastor about a new Network Marketing opportunity. Remembering the lack of success we had previously had, I was hesitant. Mary, was absolutely against it! However, God had seared my memory of our past experience. Much like a woman in labor with child number 1. She is certain that she will never go through that experience again! She only wants to kill whoever caused all of this pain she is going through. LOL! But later, somehow, she is ready to have another child. I was ready for something. Just did not know what.

Four years before that November, I had made the decision to become completely obedient to whatever God's word said and to whatever His will for my life was. I had become a 'slave to righteousness' as Romans 6:19 says. When this new opportunity came into my life, I had resolved to operate differently than I had in our previous endeavor. God honored that. I built my business on the foundation of Christ. Living out my life verse – Philippians 2:3. *"Do nothing out of selfish ambition or vain conceit, but in humility, consider others more important than yourself."* In-Network Marketing speak, it is the quote made famous by Zig Ziglar – "help enough other people get what they want, and you will get everything you want." God honored that in a big way! He will for you too. God's truth is always truth! Truth for every area of our life, in every season of our life, in every area of the world AND… in your Network Marketing business.

While building the Amway business, we had 50 people on our team after six years, with no days off! Compare that with the first six years in my current company, 8,000 had joined us over that time, and we had hit the top rank in our company. The two experiences were night and day. However, without all that we learned while having no financial success during our Amway experience, we would not have had the success we enjoy today. I say that only to say.... God's way works! *"God causes all things to work together for good for those who love Him and are called according to His purposes"* Romans 8:28.

After reaching the top rank in our company and achieving that elusive 'financial freedom' we all desire, God called me to pastor a new campus for the church we were then attending. Honestly, I did not see that coming. However, because I had previously decided to be obedient to the Lord, I said yes as He was clearly calling me to it. Through these and other circumstances, I believe that the Lord has allowed me to understand how He operates and how He wants us to walk in His will AND how all of this applies to us in our chosen businesses.

Now, why am I writing this book? I believe that if you are reading this book, you are a person of faith, or are open to it. You also desire more success in your life and probably in your business. Perhaps you have been frustrated because you see others having success and don't understand why you have not had the success you desire. That was me for three decades! Over the last 46 years, I have watched tens of thousands of people enter this industry desiring more out of life. I have had tens of thousands of conversations with people who continue to self-sabotage and/or resign themselves to a perceived reality that "this is just the way it is." The story we begin to tell ourselves goes like this – I want more success, but I don't truly believe I am going to get it. I will keep working, though. I will do enough to make myself feel better about the lack of success I am having while I hold on to the hope that one day, someone will come into my team and make me more successful. This is an awful place to be, because our belief is what drives our activity and ultimately, our results!

This book will provide deep biblical truth, foundational truth, that will allow you to fully understand that God has bigger plans for you. We will get to the "roots" of those things that hold you back. God has plans to prosper you. However, we must operate according to God's word and will. Ephesians 2:10 says that *YOU are God's workmanship (masterpiece), created in Christ Jesus to do good works, which God prepared in advance for you to do!!* When you begin walking in the truth of who and whose you are, you will walk in more confidence in your daily life. As a result, you will have more impact on more people. Not because you are so good, but because God, through His Holy Spirit, is living through you, the very life you were created to live!! Those things that God does, through those who are submitted and obedient, will feed your humility, not your pride. As you impact more people for God's purposes, more people will be influenced by you because God goes before you! Let's begin!

CHAPTER 1
Foundation On Rock

Each, and every business that begins, start's with a long-term focus. As Network Marketers, we should act in kind. Unfortunately, the overwhelming majority of those who begin in our industry do so with a very short term focus. Most, if we are honest, 'give it a try.' Because there is typically no large capital investment, there is no large effort investment. Most never consider a 'business plan' and, as a result, have no plan at all. The goal, of course, is to make money. But, people 'try' and see if they have success out of the gate. If it works, then they may continue. If those people that they thought would join them, did not, they figure that it must not be for them and back to their life they go. There was no long-term commitment or plan. By doing this, they have validated exactly why those people chose not to join them.

Very few are able to accurately count the cost for success of any kind. Since most have no understanding of what is required to lead hundreds or thousands of people, they continually count the cost along the way. They are continually re-deciding to pay the price for greater success. Jesus addressed this very topic. In Luke 14:28-32, Jesus tells a story (parable) about the building of a building and a king going to war.

Suppose one of you wants to build a tower. Won't you first sit down and estimate the cost to see if you have enough money to complete it? [29] For if you lay, the foundation and are not able to finish it, everyone who sees it will ridicule you, [30] saying, 'This person began to build and wasn't able to finish.'

[31] "Or suppose a king is about to go to war against another king. Won't he first sit down and consider whether he is able with ten thousand men to oppose the one coming against him with twenty thousand? [32] If he is not able, he will send a delegation while the other is still a long way off and will ask for terms of peace.

Now, the first story is just like our industry. Most people never meet anyone who has had success in the Network Marketing industry. Meaning, they typically aren't working directly with such a person. What most see is the person who starts without true commitment, tries, and subsequently quits. They are excited about the possibilities but have not grown strong in their conviction about what they are setting out to achieve. What happens next is just like verse 29 above – "everyone who sees it will ridicule you."

Personally, I despise this reality. It happens over and over. A person decides to undertake an endeavor to change their station in life. They go to their family and friends with their 'big news' and are immediately shut down by those closest to them. Many times...ridiculed. Why? The truth is that when one person decides to make changes, many who are close to them are then challenged in their own life. The underlying reason for the ridicule is that when Bill sees his good friend, Amy, making changes, that Bill is not ready to make, Bill wants to ensure that Amy doesn't succeed. He does this because he must protect his desire to keep the status quo. If Amy succeeds, now Bill has to wrestle with his own insecurities, failings, and self-limiting beliefs!

To be sure, Bill will never say these things. Nor will your friends. However, that is the underlying reality. It is easier for Bill to beat Amy down than to take the chance that he may have to change. Sadly, in this example, if Amy is not strong in her convictions, the ridicule will cause her to quit on her dream of a better life. No doubt, you have heard that you are the average of the nine other people you are closest to. This is because people are comfortable in that circle of people. All are at roughly the same socio-economic level in life. No one person really challenges the other(s) to get better. To grow. The conversation is simple and relatable. However, when you want to change some things in your life, you need to change some things in your life. If you have spent any time around Network Marketing, you have probably heard that you will need to either change your friends or change your friends. This can be hard for people to understand. Over the years, I have realized that we don't actually leave our friends behind. What we do is seek out those who have the mind-set that we do. If those closest to us choose not to come with us, we may have to leave their mind-set. This truth is laid out by Peter in 1 Peter 4:3,4:

For you have spent enough time in the past doing what pagans choose to do—living in debauchery, lust, drunkenness, orgies, carousing and detestable idolatry. 4 They are surprised that you do not join them in their reckless, wild living, and they heap abuse on you.

While we are not talking about wild living, the point is that when one chooses to live differently, they (those who don't come with you) are surprised and heap abuse on you! When this happens, the new network marketer thinks it is their new business that is in question. Noooo! Your friends are simply projecting their self-limiting beliefs on to you.

You don't have to accept that as your reality. People have been the same for millennia. Again, truth is truth – ALWAYS!!

Long ago, I learned about Greyhound races. To my surprise, I learned that the dogs don't actually race! They actually chase a mechanical rabbit. The rabbit is on a track around the course. The dogs simply chase, and the fastest dog wins. If there were no mechanical rabbits, the dogs would just be running in circles. When others don't see our "rabbit,"; i.e., our Dream. Goal. Idea. Vision. They think we are just running in circles. But, just because someone else does not see your rabbit, don't allow that to discourage you from pursuing it.

The key to growing your conviction is knowing where you are going, why you are going, and having a plan for getting there; Counting the cost; Give yourself time to win. Put together a good plan to get where you want to go. Get with someone you trust, who has your best interest in mind, and has the experience going where you want to go. To put a good plan in place, you must have specific action steps and dates to make a goal, a goal. With no plan and date, you simply have a wish.

Jesus told the parable of building on rock in Matthew 7:24-27. He was wrapping up what is known as the sermon on the mount. After providing many "how to's" on living life well, he said:

"Therefore, everyone who hears these words of mine and puts them into practice is like a wise man who built his house on the rock.
25 The rain came down, the streams rose, and the winds blew and beat against that house, yet it did not fall, because it had its foundation on the rock. 26 But everyone who hears these words of mine and does not put them into practice is like a foolish man who built his house on sand. 27 The rain came down, the streams rose, and the winds blew and beat against that house, and it fell with a great crash."

Why is this parable relevant to your business? As you set goals, you must begin with the end in mind. Always play for the long term. To achieve great success, the success that you want, you must build teams. Building teams requires time, relationships, helping others through their struggles, helping them overcome their leadership lids, etc. If you are just out to make a buck or two, then you will be tempted to do things that benefit you, but hurt others. That is building your business on sand.

As you build, know what standard you are going to operate under. For me, that standard is set by Christ. Loving others, doing good to all, extending grace, forgiving, etc. That said, if you are going to lead a large team, you must have a big and solid vision. We will cover more of that in later chapters. The non-negotiables for growing large teams are integrity, commitment, and honesty. A lack of vision can be overcome early if you do what you say you are going to do and never waiver! James, the brother of Jesus, referred this in James 5:12 - *But most of all, my brothers and sisters, never take an oath, by heaven or earth or anything else. Just say a simple yes or no, so that you will not sin and be condemned.*

Paul also referred to this when writing to the church in Corinth in 2 Cor. 2:17 - *You may be asking why I changed my plan. Do you think I make my plans carelessly? Do you think I am like people of the world who say "Yes" when they really mean "No"?*

Paul and James operated at a different standard. We should do the same. When you make a commitment, keep it! Period! A great standard that will be of great help to you is this – 'whatever is best for my team, is best for me.' This was my rule from day one. Unfortunately, over the past ten years of building, I have violated that rule twice. It bit me both times! Never again! Never do anything that you will have to apologize for later. This is building on rock. There are certain ethical standards that you will not violate. If you commit to such things early, you will always have the rule in place to operate under. When you do this, you will not have to make leadership decisions on the fly. You can put each situation that arises under the microscope of your 'standard.' Hopefully, that is God's standard as well. It will eliminate much stress as you build. When we do things God's way, He takes on the responsibility for the outcome. Wow! What a great partner our God is!

He knows everything that the future holds. He knows who you need to meet. He knows the good works you have been designed for and the works that only YOU will do. Ref. Eph. 2:10.

Building on rock and allowing Jesus to order your steps – Psalms 37:23 - *The steps of a good man are ordered by the LORD, And He delights in his way.* – You can rest assured that God's Holy Spirit will lead you where you need to be and to whom you need to know. When you learn to walk in God's truth, you will walk with bold humility. You will KNOW that God will do what He says He will do. That kind of confidence is attractive to others.
Build your foundation on rock, The Rock.
Jesus Christ.

Chapter 2
Jesus, the First Networker

While Jesus' purpose was far greater than simply connecting with people, we can learn some incredibly powerful lessons from His life. And, as a pastor, I would never want to minimize the ultimate purpose for Jesus' coming to earth. He came to die for our sins so that we could be reconciled back to God. To have right standing with God by simply believing that Jesus lived a sinless life, died for our sins and then rose again on the third day. In His overcoming death, He allows us to do the same. Praise God for that!! That said, let's learn networking secrets from the greatest networker and leader of all time.

He Believed in His product.

There is no doubt that Jesus was sure of why He was here. He had the greatest message ever known. Because He believed so heavily in His 'product', He spent every waking minute promoting it. Note: that was after 30 years of living on earth as what would have appeared to others as a normal life. Don't miss this. Ecclesiastes echoes that to everything there is a season. Once Jesus stepped into His 'season,' He gave it everything He had. Yes, His very life. Most people are not ready to give everything they have when they join a business like ours. Most need to get a greater understanding of their product, system, people, message, etc. Will cover more of this in later chapters.

You must be sold out on what you are providing – beyond the product. You must understand why your product/message improves the lives of others that it can make a positive difference in the lives of those who buy or buy-in. If you don't have this fundamental belief, you will simply be trying to make a sale to make a dollar. People see right through this. You will find it difficult to get long term growth if this is your intention. People are ok buying. Most don't want to be sold. When you fully believe in what you are doing/providing, you can simply share with others. Your belief will be transferred to others who are ready to hear from you. Then, you will experience great success in finding a customer and team members that will buy into your vision.

You see, if all you do is 'sell,' long term growth is hard. In most sales transactions, it is simply that – transactional. You make the sale and are off to the next 'sale.' Perhaps you get referrals. That is great. In most cases, once the sale is made, the relationship ends. When you intend to build a Network Marketing business or any business that requires ongoing sales, then the first sale is the beginning of the relationship, not the end. This is why you must be sold, yourself, on the value you are bringing to others.

Are you a product of your product? Do you truly use it? Does it improve the quality of your life? Are you certain that it can improve the quality of other people's lives? Do you live that out? Do others see you living it out? Remember, *a double-minded man (woman) is unstable in all his (her) ways.* James 1:8

He Invited Others To Come With Him

We call this the Recruiting process. Jesus was intentional in going out to find His early followers. Once His ministry (season) began, he began looking for a team of people that could carry on His message after He was gone. He did not wait for them to come and find Him. There is example after example of this in the Gospels. Andrew did seek Jesus out on day one when John the Baptist pointed out who Jesus was. However, when Jesus was ready to build His team, it began. Mark 1:16-20:

16 As Jesus walked beside the Sea of Galilee, he saw Simon and his brother Andrew casting a net into the lake, for they were fishermen. 17 "Come, follow me," Jesus said, "and I will send you out to fish for people." [18] *At once, they left their nets and followed him.*

[19] *When he had gone a little farther, he saw James son of Zebedee and his brother John in a boat, preparing their nets.* [20] *Without delay, he called them, and they left their father Zebedee in the boat with the hired men and followed him.*

Please note that Jesus had already built a relationship with these men. He had spent time with them, eaten at Peter's home, and performed several miracles. The account in Luke chapters 4 & 5 confirms this. None the less, Jesus continued to go out to find more followers, converts, and believers. This is exactly what we do as we go out sharing our product or idea or opportunity with others. We are simply looking for those who see it as we do. While I fully believe that God already knows who will join you, I also fully believe that they will not come knocking at your door, asking you to share your new opportunity with them.

So, get comfortable knowing that like every business that has ever started for all of history, you need someone to buy. i.e., customers. Traditional businesses will use marketing strategies, advertisements, and now social media to get their message out. What message? Hey, we are open for business and looking for customers! In our industry, it is slightly different. We, individually, are the marketing arm. So, you need to go out and personally find some people who are looking for what you have. It begins with a list of names of people you know. Don't be intimidated by this. The names list is your raw material. If you have people to share with, you are always in business. Once you sponsor an initial group of people, Jesus started with 12, then begin to know who they know. And voila! You are building a team.

Again, Jesus did this very thing with Matthew (Levi) and Zacchaeus. He went out and met them, called them, and then had a party to get to know their friends.

Luke 5:27-29 - *27 After this, Jesus went out and saw a tax collector by the name of Levi sitting at his tax booth. "Follow me," Jesus said to him, 28 and Levi got up, left everything and followed him.29 Then Levi held a great banquet for Jesus at his house, and a large crowd of tax collectors and others were eating with them.*

Jesus went out, met Levi, put him in on his team, and then began meeting some of his friends. This may sound familiar. It is exactly what we do in our businesses. Jesus perfected it!

Luke 19:5,6 - [5] *When Jesus reached the spot, he looked up and said to him, "Zacchaeus, come down immediately. I must stay at your house today." [6] So he came down at once and welcomed him gladly.*

Interestingly, they were both tax collectors. Both had money and influence. As you are recruiting, look for those who have credibility as well. This will help your team grow faster. However, I have found that the most important trait someone can have is hunger! A strong desire for a different life. As you meet and involve people in your business, always look for those that have a hunger for more. Learn to meet the people that other people know. Again, your belief, as outlined above, will allow you to do this with confidence.

People Quit

As with many things in life, people quit. They quit jobs, school, marriages, relationships, and yes, Network Marketing businesses! You must learn to accept that not everyone who begins with you will finish with you. It is just not reality. Too many people allow this one thing to take them out. You know this scenario.... Andy sees your opportunity and is excited about it.

He goes out and shares with a few people and runs into some rejection, and quickly, he is ready to quit. You had your hopes way up because Andy had great potential. You thought you had someone that would be successful, which would make you more money. Then, when he fell away, you allow that to impact your own belief and enthusiasm. You must, must learn to control your emotional attachment to yes', no's aces, quitters, talkers, etc. Simply make the decision that you are going to win. Decide to do what it takes to achieve your goal and resolve to do the work!

I liken this to something called 'micro-trauma.' If you have ever made a decision to get into shape, join a gym, start exercising again after some time off, you have experienced this. When we overwork a muscle, we tear muscle fiber. Our body begins to repair it. Lactic acid is produced when the muscles tear. That is the burn you feel in your muscles when you begin exercising again or for the first time. Personal trainers will refer to this as 'micro-trauma.' The individual cells are small. Many small cells with micro-trauma can add up to a lot of pain. Many, many people who feel this pain abandon their desire for a better physique. The micro-trauma overcomes the macro-vision they had of getting into better shape. In our world, people get hurt by those who don't see our opportunity like we do. Specifically, those that start and quit. Most people allow that pain – micro-trauma – to cause them to give up on their new-found dream of financial freedom or whatever it might be. Their 'macro-vision.' Don't let this be you.

Jesus experienced people quitting in droves! The most famous, of course, is Judas Iscariot, who ultimately betrayed Jesus to the Sanhedrin and Pilate. However, that betrayal occurred on the last day of Jesus' earthly ministry. Prior to that, many walked away because they found the cost of following too great.

John 6:60-66 - *60 On hearing it, many of his disciples said, "This is a hard teaching. Who can accept it?"61 Aware that his disciples were grumbling about this, Jesus said to them, "Does this offend you? 62 Then what if you see the Son of Man ascend to where he was before! 63 The Spirit gives life; the flesh counts for nothing. The words I have spoken to you— they are full of the Spirit[e] and life. 64 Yet there are some of you who do not believe." For Jesus had known from the beginning, which of them did not believe and who would betray him. 65 He went on to say, "This is why I told you that no one can come to me unless the Father has enabled them."66 From this time, many of his disciples turned back and <u>no longer followed him.</u>*

If people are going to quit on the greatest message ever told by the greatest leader ever known, they will quit your team as well. Don't think this is an issue with you, your opportunity, or message. No doubt, there may need to be work to be done in those areas. But, realize that people have been quitting things forever. It is what people do.

One other incident that Jesus had encountered involved a young rich man. Don't miss the truth of this encounter. It is outlined in Mark 10:17-23

17 As Jesus started on his way, a man ran up to him and fell on his knees before him. "Good teacher," he asked, "what must I do to inherit eternal life?"18 "Why do you call me good?" Jesus answered. "No one is good—except God alone. 19 You know the commandments: 'You shall not murder, you shall not commit adultery, you shall not steal, you shall not give false testimony, you shall not defraud, honor your father and mother.'[d]"20 "Teacher," he declared, "all these I have kept since I was a boy."21 Jesus looked at him and loved him. "One thing you lack," he said. "Go, sell everything you have and give to the poor, and you will have treasure in heaven. Then come, follow me."22 At this, the man's face fell. He went away sad because he had great wealth.23 Jesus looked around and said to his disciples, "How hard it is for the rich to enter the kingdom of God!"

Many people use this passage to say that wealth is bad. IT IS NOT! Having money was never an issue with Jesus. It is when money has us that we get into trouble. It can become an idol. In the case of the man who came to Jesus, his money was very important to him. That is true, but it is not the principle I want you to see here. You see, Jesus shared with the man what he must do to be saved. The man chose not to do that and "went away sad." AND JESUS LET HIM!! Understand that Jesus never begged anyone to follow Him. When they chose not to, Jesus let them walk away from the greatest message ever. You must do the same. When people quit, when they say no, just know that they are not who you need in your life. Don't get discouraged over it. Simply continue on with your mission, just like Jesus did.

As a matter of fact, Jesus specifically tells the story of a great banquet that explains what happens to many of us today. You know, when people tell you they will do one thing and then don't. Hopefully, you will be able to take comfort from this story.

Jesus spoke to them again in parables, saying: "The kingdom of heaven is like a king who prepared a wedding banquet for his son. He sent his servants to those who had been invited to the banquet to tell them to come, but they refused to come. "Then he sent some more servants and said, 'Tell those who have been invited that I have prepared my dinner: My oxen and fattened cattle have been butchered, and everything is ready. Come to the wedding banquet.' "But they paid no attention and went off—one to his field, another to his business. "Then he said to his servants, 'The wedding banquet is ready, but those I invited did not deserve to come. So go to the street corners and invite to the banquet anyone you find.' So the servants went out into the streets and gathered all the people they could find, the bad as well as the good, and the wedding hall was filled with guests. Mat. 22:1-10

Let me just say, during the time when Jesus tells this story when the king is going to have a banquet, and you are invited; you show up! The food will be different than what was eaten daily by those invited. But even still, as great as that event would have been, people made excuses and bowed out, one-by-one. So, the king begins to invite others to replace them. Don't miss the lessons here. First, people will disappoint you. Many will say that they will do something and then not do that thing. Don't allow a lack of integrity in someone else to impact where you are going. They weren't meant to go on your journey with you! I love what Jesus says in v. 8 – *"those I invited did not deserve to come."* You should have that same mindset.

Secondly, the king was not deterred. He invited others. Too many times, I hear this statement, which is absolutely, false; "the ones you think will say yes, won't, and the ones you think will say no, will say yes." Listen close…YOU DON'T KNOW who will say yes or no. So, ask many. Invite many. Here is some wise inviting advice; "say less to more people." Let those who are looking for what you have found you by inviting many people to look.

He Loved People

Obviously, Jesus loved people. It was more than what He did; it is who He was/is. God is Love. Jesus is the exact representation of God. Therefore, He is love as well. We need to learn how to love people, as well. Truly love them. Today, my mantra is "Love 'em and Lead 'em." I love everyone and lead those that are ready to be led. You should consider this same approach. It will eliminate stress from your life. Not everyone is ready to participate in your endeavor with you. Be ok with that. After all, we are really an interruption in people's lives. We come along like Jesus did, and invite others to join us. Some are ready for an interruption, and some are not. Everyone is ready to be loved though. 1 Corinthians 13:4-7 gives us the practical definition of what love is:

Love is patient, love is kind. It does not envy, it does not boast, it is not proud. [5] It does not dishonor others, it is not self-seeking, it is not easily angered, it keeps no record of wrongs. [6] Love does not delight in evil but rejoices with the truth. [7] It always protects, always trusts, always hopes, always perseveres.

Love is always a choice. Read the passage again. We can choose to love or not. When you love others, you always have their best interest in mind. People in your life will never find that offensive. So, again love everyone. Lead those that are ready to go with you. Loving people sometimes means that you may need to exhort them, correct them, challenge them, and forgive them. As your team grows, you will learn when to do what. Over time, as you love and lead others through various life circumstances, you learn what is needed at the right time.

In businesses like ours, most people will have mentors that you can speak with when necessary. People who have already traveled the road that you are currently traveling. Use that experience to help you be a more effective leader.

Jesus Built His People Up

"Build the People, and the People Build the Business"
- Dexter Yager, Founder's Crown Ambassador, Amway

Helping others grow is probably the most difficult part of leadership. We can learn to love people relatively easily. Sometimes, that is done from a distance. However, if you are going to build others up, you must get up close and personal. Long ago, during my Amway days, I had a conversation with Dexter Yager, who is the most successful Network Marketer of all time, he told me that if we would build the people, the people will build the business. Dexter was a strong follower of Christ, as well.

Jesus spent three years predominately with the 12 Disciples. Of course, He impacted others. His primary focus was building a small group of men, who could then go out and build others. This, of course, is our model in Network Marketing. You will not be able to effectively mentor a large number of people. We can always provide an encouraging word

to all people. From a stage, you can impress
people. To impact them, to build them, you
must invest time and energy in others.
Because of the time required, the number of
people you can truly build up (mentor) is
limited. Even in Jesus' case, He had the 12.
However, he spent more time with Peter,
James & John. You will find the same thing.
Your inner circle will determine much of your
success. Be vigilant in investing your time with
the right people. You only have so much of it.
Not all will succeed or even stay with you. But
you will never be sorry when helping others to
grow because you grow through that process.

If you want to go fast, go alone. If you want to
go far, go together! Success in our industry will
always be determined by the team you
assemble. Resolve to be like Jesus in this
area. Build up others. They will want to be
around you when you make them feel better
about themselves. If you are always tearing
others down, you will have an organization of
dwarfs. If you are always building others up,
you will have an organization of giants!

Explained the cost

Jesus never shied away from telling people that following Him would cost them. He used some pretty strong language in Luke 14:25-27

[25] *Large crowds were traveling with Jesus, and turning to them he said:* [26] *"If anyone comes to me and does not hate father and mother, wife and children, brothers and sisters—yes, even their own life—such a person cannot be my disciple.* [27] *And whoever does not carry their cross and follow me cannot be my disciple.*

And again:

Matthew 8:21,22 - *Another disciple said to him, "Lord, first let me go and bury my father."* [22] *But Jesus told him, "Follow me, and let the dead bury their own dead."*

Only a small percentage of all of those who enter into the Network Marketing industry will actually do what it takes to build a large organization. Most will do a minimal amount and wonder why they are not attaining greater success. They will not pay the price that success demands. For those who do desire to have that higher level of success, it is vital that, at some point, a decision to pay the price is made. To do that, people must understand the cost. You, as a leader, need to be ready to clearly outline the cost to those who are ready. If you are the person who needs to understand the cost, get to someone who has already had success in the area where you desire success. Ask them to be honest in telling you what is required. Then, you get to decide how you move forward.

A similar conversation can be had when one wants to set a short-term goal. Perhaps, one is ready to take a smaller step toward greater success. Awesome! The cost for that incremental step is still vital to understand. I have found that few people can really see the 'end' result, whether it be great notoriety or financial freedom or whatever it might be. If you are that person who can see the big picture and commit to a multi-year journey, you are unique. You are a person that can impact many, many others who will follow you. I want to encourage you to go after your dream with everything in you. If you are not that person, be sure to break the journey into smaller steps. As you do, you will grow as a person and leader. Concurrently, your vision will grow, which will, in turn, change the words you speak to yourself and others. This process is invaluable!

Tere Kampe

He Cast vision

Because the price to follow Jesus in the first century A.D. was so high, Jesus was constantly casting vision to His disciples. He was constantly explaining the reward for the following.

Luke 12:4-8 - *4 "I tell you, my friends, do not be afraid of those who kill the body and after that can do no more. 5 But I will show you whom you should fear: Fear him who, after your body has been killed, has authority to throw you into hell. Yes, I tell you, fear him. 6 Are not five sparrows sold for two pennies? Yet not one of them is forgotten by God. 7 Indeed, the very hairs of your head are all numbered. Don't be afraid; you are worth more than many sparrows.8 "I tell you, whoever publicly acknowledges me before others, the Son of Man will also acknowledge before the angels of God.*

Luke 12:29-31 - *29 And do not set your heart on what you will eat or drink; do not worry about it. 30 For the pagan world runs after all such things, and your Father knows that you need them. 31 But seek his kingdom, and these things will be given to you as well.*

John 14:1-3 - *"Do not let your hearts be troubled. You believe in God[a]; believe also in me. ² My Father's house has many rooms; if that were not so, would I have told you that I am going there to prepare a place for you? ³ And if I go and prepare a place for you, I will come back and take you to be with me that you also may be where I am.*

Acts 1:7,8 - *⁷ He said to them: "It is not for you to know the times or dates the Father has set by his own authority. ⁸ But you will receive power when the Holy Spirit comes on you; and you will be my witnesses in Jerusalem, and in all Judea and Samaria, and to the ends of the earth."*

Vision casting may be the most under-utilized skill in Network Marketing. People are constantly facing problems in their own life or the lives of others, rejection, and disappointment based on missed expectations. As a result, people need to develop strong intestinal and mental fortitude. They must continually remember what they are working towards. Vision is caught, not taught. Jesus knew it. You should do it. If you don't yet know how to cast vision, listen to some of the top leaders that you are in business with. They will speak a different language than everyone else. In my business, I have often said that you can put several top leaders on stage. They will typically finish each other's sentences.

Regardless of how successful a person is, they must constantly be reminded of what is ahead. The moment you have nothing more to achieve is the moment you start heading back to where you started. You only coast downhill! Vision of a greater future is the key to continued accomplishment. It is what provides energy. This skill is so important, I have dedicated a full chapter to it.

Organized teams

In our industry, personally sponsoring rarely equates to success. Building teams is what pays. You must grasp this truth. The question that becomes critical is whether or not you are willing to invest in building those teams. Two different times, Jesus sent the disciples out and gave them a plan to follow.

Luke 9:1-6 - *When Jesus had called the Twelve together, he gave them power and authority to drive out all demons and to cure diseases, 2 and he sent them out to proclaim the kingdom of God and to heal the sick. 3 He told them: "Take nothing for the journey—no staff, no bag, no bread, no money, no extra shirt. 4 Whatever house you enter, stay there until you leave that town. 5 If people do not welcome you, leave their town and shake the dust off your feet as a testimony against* them." *6 So they set out and went from village to village, proclaiming the good news and healing people everywhere.*

Luke:10:1-12 - *After this, the Lord appointed seventy-two others and sent them two by two ahead of him to every town and place where he was about to go. 2 He told them, "The harvest is plentiful, but the workers are few. Ask the Lord of the harvest, therefore, to send out workers into his harvest field. 3 Go! I am sending you out like lambs among wolves. 4 Do not take a purse or bag or sandals; and do not greet anyone on the road.5 "When you enter a house, first say, 'Peace to this house.' 6 If someone who promotes peace is there, your peace will rest on them; if not, it will return to you. 7 Stay there, eating and drinking whatever they give you, for the worker deserves his wages. Do not move around from house to house.8 "When you enter a town and are welcomed, eat what is offered to you. 9 Heal the sick who are there and tell them, 'The kingdom of God has come near to you.' 10 But when you enter a town and are not welcomed, go into its streets and say, 11 'Even the dust of your town we wipe from our feet as a warning to you. Yet be sure of this: The kingdom of God has come near.' 12 I tell you, it will be more bearable on that day for Sodom than for that town.*

Jesus initially sent His inner circle of guys out. He sent the 12 so that they could experience more than they understood. Their belief grew as a result. The next time, he sent out a larger team – 72. However, he had already prepared the 12. By doing so, they could lead to smaller teams. Their prior experience helped to provide an example to the larger number. This is such a great example of how to build teams. Teach some to teach some. As your teams grow, you will find that you will spend more of your time building the leaders, so that they can build the teams. Even Jesus, who was fully God, was also fully man, did this. Being fully man meant that He only had 24 hours each day. Humanly speaking, we are limited in the number of people we can actually and effectively build into. Jesus chose 12. You must do the same who you surround yourself with matters. The stronger your inner circle, the stronger the team.

Keep in mind, you must continue to grow yourself as a leader if you want to have stronger leaders follow you! It is a never-ending process. However, the payoff is well worth it. Note, I am not referring only to a financial reward. I am referring to a fulfillment that comes from watching others grow in their own lives. Helping others overcome self-limiting beliefs and fears, so that they step into the greatness that is within them. When this occurs, you will find that success will give way to significance. Your focus will shift from gaining more for yourself to helping others attain more in their lives! This is when the work of building teams really pays off. There are numerous books on the topic of leadership and team building. Fill your mind with the experience and knowledge of other successful people on this topic.

He Gave everything he had

Obviously, Jesus gave His life to fulfill His purpose. Most of us will not have to give our life to be successful. That said, those who do achieve extraordinary success do make it their life's mission. And, that is the difference. I remember, about one year into my current business, I had attended an Entrepreneur/Leadership seminar. During that event, the main speaker spoke of the balance wheel of life. You know, a wheel has many spokes. In the wheel of life, the spokes represent various aspects of your life - social, spiritual, relational, financial, physical, professional, etc. As he spoke that day, I realized that what I do fulfills EVERY aspect of life. Not only did it fulfill my life, but I could also impact others in every one of those areas! At that moment, my business stopped being "what I did" and became "who I am"!!

In that instant, I knew I could give everything to my business because it fulfilled the purpose, for which, God put me on the earth. I could pursue the highest levels in our company not because it paid well, but because I knew it would only be a byproduct of making a positive difference in the lives of thousands of people. As a believer in Christ, I have learned that our true purpose is to know God and make Him known! In helping many other people improve their social, spiritual, or whatever aspect of their life that needs help, I could live out my life verse – Philippians 2:3 – considering others more important than myself. By doing that, I could live out Christ right in front of them. Hopefully, they would see more of Christ and less of me. Just like John the Baptist said in John 3:30 – *"He must become greater, I must become less."*

If there is one thing that I could wish for you, it would be that your heart and mind come into full agreement with the other and with God's will for your life. When that happens, you will be free to give everything to what you believe in. You will never have to apologize to anyone, anytime. You will be completely whole, and you will be able to give everything, as Jesus did because it is who you are!

I regularly speak with people who 'want' more success in their Network Marketing business.

Since you are reading this, you are probably one of them. The challenge I constantly see and hear is that they have never truly gone all in. For example, when someone asks you what you do, is your first answer what you do as a business (particularly if you are still working a day job), or is it your day job? Invariably, it is what they do as an occupation. Their 'business' is their 'side-hustle.' You know, this little thing I do on the side. Ahhh!! No one will follow that lack of conviction. Whether you are fulltime or not, if you want success - greater success – you must get sold out to what you do. It should always be your number one answer to the question.... 'what do you do for work?'.

Once I realized that my endeavor was who I am, I was finally whole. The best word is "integrity." One definition of integrity is – a state of being whole. This is such a great place to be. You have full integrity in your life. When you don't, you are dis-integrated. A definition of disintegrate is - to separate into parts or lose intactness or solidness; break up; deteriorate. Think about this in your life. If you lack solidness or intactness, you are divided. Jesus said in Mark 3:25 - *If a house is divided against itself, that house cannot stand.*

You desire to have others follow you. Until you are ready to give everything to your chosen endeavor, don't expect many to go with you. Humanly speaking, people are really interested in things that benefit themselves. If they are going to follow you, they need to believe that you can help them get what they want out of life. If you aren't committed enough to be all in, they will certainly not believe that following you is the answer.

Chapter 3
Proper Mindset

May I just say, I absolutely love talking about mindset! The set of your mind will determine what you will and won't accomplish in life. An important thing that you need to understand right up front – You are exactly where you want to be in life. Now, some of you may argue this statement. However, the more you understand about why this is true, the more you will agree with it. Here is the very liberating part of this truth…. Because you are exactly where you want to be, you can go anywhere you choose! How can this be?

You see, every choice that you have made was based on how you perceive yourself. You may have heard this described as your self-image. More to the point, it is the way you imagine yourself. You will always fulfill the image you have of yourself. This reality affects every area of your life, from the relationships to your financial situation. Unfortunately, until we realize that we have any control in this very important area, we won't change it. Most of what has formed our self-image comes from what happened to us and what was said to us in our younger years.

Someone had our keyboard when we were growing up. They were writing code in our minds. As we experienced different things in life, our reality was formed. If you were brought up in a home where you heard something like "money is the root of all evil," you may have an aversion to making a large amount of money. Now, this statement is not true. It is a misquote of the bible verse, which states that "*the LOVE of money is A root of all kinds of evil*." 1 Timothy 6:10. Regardless of the truth of the statement, if that message went into your mind enough and took root, it has become part of your mindset. This, in turn, impacted your belief system and impacts your self-image. i.e. if you believe that money is evil and you do not want to be an evil person, you will ensure that you don't have an amount of money that is more than what you think (believe) is not evil. What?? Don't miss this. There is no specific amount. However, you will develop this amount based on your experience of life. It will probably be an amount that creates a lifestyle much like your parents had.

I had to come to grips with the fact that I had a low bar of financial success. This did not become clear until I was 48 years old. I very much dislike that I was 48 before I recognized this. Let's look at how this plays out. See if you relate - Early on, I mentioned that my parents were in Amway for 43 years. My dad saw Amway as a way to get out of computer programming back in the early '70s. A few years in, they had achieved the first level of success there and had some seemingly good things going on in their business. So, he made the choice to leave his job at roughly 38 years old. Never having been involved in the Network Marketing industry, he was not aware of the ups and downs. My parents never achieved higher ranks. Back in the day, they blew out the walls in the house to add a couple of rooms. One was the stock room. They carried about $60,000 in inventory at the house. That was when $60,000 meant something. As a result, while we had an immense amount of love in our home – my parents were the coolest parents around. Ours was the gathering place for all of our friends, mostly because my parents were home due to the relative freedom that they had – we never had that "successful money."

They never really achieved time freedom. They were always working hard in their business. That is not a bad thing. But the idea of financial freedom or time freedom never came. At least, in my eyes. As I saw it, they were the people that worked hard to help the successful people become successful. This is why I never wanted to join the business. I saw it a lot of work without much reward.

In the introduction, I mentioned that I ultimately did join. This was because through the leaders they were following, they got connected to Dexter Yager, mentioned earlier. Dexter is literally the number one income earner in all of Network Marketing for all companies, for all time. His philosophy of building was completely different, and it made sense to me. So, I jumped all in! Candidly, I was psychotic about it. I was so excited because I thought I had found the way to get to that financial freedom I had heard so much about for 20 years. I had great enthusiasm, but apparently, lacked leadership ability. Our results were abysmal. Truly. This may give you hope. Honestly, over a 6-year period, I never took one day off from either showing our opportunity to someone or being out trying to find someone to show it to. After roughly 2200 days, and at least 1700 presentations to at least 2500 people, we had 50 people on our team. That equates to 1 of every 50 people I showed. Lol, that is not a good closing ratio. So, after six years, I came to the conclusion that either the opportunity did not work or "I sucked at it." Others were having success during that same time. So, I decided it was me – and quit. I assumed that real financial freedom was for 'other' people. Not me. Not my family. Note: this is not truth. It was the set of my mind. Otherwise known as mindset. I returned my focus to my job and made the best life I could with that.

Thirteen years later, a new opportunity was introduced to me. I respected the friend that showed me, but my past results were firmly planted in my mind. My first inclination was to help my friend get out of this idea he was showing me. Why? Because I did not have success earlier in life. I wanted to save him the pain and discouragement! I was trying to put my self-limiting beliefs on him. And that is what your friends and family members do to you. Every time they try to talk you out of following your dream, they are really telling you that they are afraid to try. Ahhhh! In our industry, these people are known as 'dream stealers.' Since they don't have the desire to change their situation, they want to ensure you don't either. These are people you need to be on high alert for.

Wow, ok, back to my story. You see, because I had only experienced failure (at least, that is how I saw it) and had seen limited success in my parents' business, that was my 'reality.' Based on my own experience. However, I did one thing right while I was considering my current business. I prayed. I asked God to confirm that I should or should not pursue it. God allowed me to see my past from a different perspective. I had only seen it as failure. God allowed me to reframe it to see it as preparation! That was huge. I suddenly understood that all the years of fruitless effort wasn't really fruitless at all. But, as long as that was my mindset, that was truth to me. In changing my perspective, it allowed me to understand that my truth was not the actual truth. I hope that makes sense. This is so big! This is the thing that drives everything in your life.

I like to equate our mindset, a.k.a. the set of your mind, to a toolset, that a carpenter might use. Decades ago, when a carpenter wanted to drive nails into wood, he would get his hammer out and start pounding away. With such tools, many millions of homes were built. Then, with the introduction of nail guns, that same job is accomplished with much less effort and greater efficiency. Now, there is a nail gun for all sorts of jobs. They have been further refined to make every job easier. The tool-set that a carpenter has allows him to get more accomplished faster. Similarly, our mind-set can make our success come faster or slower based on the tools that it contains. In the case of mind-set, the tools are; self-talk, financial astuteness, our comfort zones, self-discipline, self-image, and the list goes on. If we are trying to solve 12th-grade problems with 6th-grade thinking, we are going to struggle. Likewise, if you are trying to get to an annual income of $250,000, but employing habits and thinking of a person who earns $40,000/yr,

you must be open to changing your thinking.
i.e., your mindset.

As mentioned earlier in this chapter, much of
our self-image comes from early life
experiences. Later in life, when we fulfill the
picture we have of ourselves, it only confirms
that we are who we think we are – how we see
ourselves. Our identity is found in our past.
God wants us to get our identity in Christ.
Understanding who we are in Christ and the
power that resides in us will radically change
your perspective on who you are. Here are
some truths from God's word:
You are a Child of God!

John 1:12 - *Yet to all who did receive him, to
those who believed in his name, he gave the
right to become children of God*

Romans 8:14 - *For those who are led by the
Spirit of God are the children of God.*

Romans 8:37 - *No, in all these things we are
more than conquerors through him who loved
us.*

Galatians 4:7 - *So you are no longer a slave,
but God's child; and since you are his child,
God has made you also an heir.*

You are an Overcomer

1 John 5:4 - *for everyone born of God overcomes the world. This is the victory that has overcome the world, even our faith.*

You have the Power that Raised Christ!

Eph. 1:18-20 - *I pray that the eyes of your heart may be enlightened in order that you may know the hope to which he has called you, the riches of his glorious inheritance in his holy people, and his <u>incomparably great power for us who believe. That power is the same as the mighty strength</u> <u>he exerted when he raised Christ from the dead</u> and seated him at his right hand in the heavenly realms….*

We are more than we know. God knows who He created you to be. Allow the truth of His word to penetrate your heart and mind. Here is the mental picture that helps me. First, Paul urges us to put on the *helmet of salvation* – Ephesians 6:17. Once we have salvation, meaning we believe that Jesus died for our sins, then we can bring every *thought captive under Christ* – 2 Corinthians 10:5. We can do this because *we have the mind of Christ* – 1 Corinthians 2:16.

In my mind, I picture putting on the helmet of salvation, so that my mind is protected from the enemy, therefore, since I now have access to the Holy Spirit (the mind of Christ), I can take each thought that comes in – taking it captive – and make it obedient to Christ. Meaning, I can discern the thought, ask for wisdom on where that thought comes from, apply God's word and truth to it, and see if it lines up with God's word and will. Once done, I can choose how to move forward. If it all passes the test, I have full confidence to move. If it does not pass, then I know it is coming from a source other than God. That could be the enemy twisting the truth, or it could be my own self-limiting belief playing out in my thought-life.

If you understand what you just read and apply it in your own life, you can be set free from your past mistakes, failures, experiences, etc. You see, this process doesn't only apply to real-time happenings. Understanding this will allow you to ask the God who knows all to shed His truth on all thinking – present or past! Once you see all through God's wisdom, you can see actual truth, not just your truth, based on your limited thinking and understanding! This was life-changing to me once I finally understood that God truly wanted to participate in EVERY area of my life. In Jeremiah 33:3 – God says, "call to me and I will answer you and tell you the great and unsearchable things you do not know." Also....

Tere Kampe

James 1:5-8 - *If any of you lacks wisdom, you should ask God, who gives generously to all without finding fault, and it will be given to you. ⁶ But when you ask, you must believe and not doubt, because the one who doubts is like a wave of the sea, blown and tossed by the wind. ⁷ That person should not expect to receive anything from the Lord. ⁸ Such a person is double-minded and unstable in all they do.*

I love the James passage because God is saying…. When you need wisdom, ask me. I will give it to you without holding your past against you. Ahhhh!! That is great news! However, many times we stumble in verse 6 – you know, the "must believe and not doubt" part. Too many times, we believe we can handle our situation. We know what to do. So, we may throw up a light prayer for help, but then we go try to fix our situation with the same thinking that got us into the situation. That, my friend, is being double-minded! Asking God for wisdom but relying on our own. The crazy part of that is that when that happens, we actually blame God for not getting us out of the situation when our own thinking isn't successful. You might want to read that again. Particularly, verse 7.

I have seen it over and over. People say they want answers from God. They say that they pray. The reality is, what WE want is the outcome WE want. Most times, God has other plans. God's ways are not our ways:

Isaiah 55:8,9 - *"For my thoughts are not your thoughts, neither are your ways my ways,"* declares the LORD.[9] *"As the heavens are higher than the earth, so are my ways higher than your ways and my thoughts than your thoughts."*

Know this: God's desire for our life as a follower of Christ is to look more like Christ every day. Therefore, since we know that Romans 8:28 tells us that *"we know that in all things God works for the good of those who love him, who[i] have been called according to his purpose.* We know that God has our best interest in mind. Our best interest, in God's eyes, is for us to look like Christ. Soooo, God uses all kinds of circumstances to form us, mold us, shape us. Further Ephesians 1:11 tells us - *In him we were also chosen, having been predestined according to the plan of him who works out everything in conformity with the purpose of his will,*

What is His will? First, that all would come to salvation. 2 Peter 3:9 - *The Lord is not slow in keeping his promise, as some understand* *slowness. Instead, he is patient with you, not wanting anyone to perish, but <u>everyone to come to repentance</u>.*

Secondly, once we believe that Jesus died for our sins, and have salvation, God's will for us is found in 1 Thessalonians 4:3 - *It is God's will that you should be <u>sanctified</u>: that you should avoid sexual immorality;* Being sanctified is being made holy. i.e., look more like Christ.

About this time, you may be wondering how all of this relates to mindset. Well, I am glad you asked. Ready? Much written and spoken on the topic of 'success' or 'self-help' or 'Positive Mental Attitude' falls short of the foundational truth of who we are. Most don't or won't touch on the spiritual part of humans. Oh, they touch on it in a kind of ethereal way. If you will meditate or get in touch with your spirit, or get your energy just right so that you vibrate at the right frequency to attract all that you want from the universe.

I say – it is all crap! We are all created beings. That means there is a Creator. The "universe" will never answer you. That is a humanistic perspective which puts us at the center, instead of God. The problem is, when you come to the end of yourself, you have no other source to draw from. As a Christ-follower, I speak with the Creator of the universe! When you truly know who you are and whose you are, everything changes. God's word, as outlined above, provides truth for each and every circumstance that we walkthrough. We can know, with certainty, that the God who created everything by breathing it into existence, is the same God that lives in you through His Holy Spirit! That Spirit is our counselor, as Jesus put it in John 16:13 - *But when he, the Spirit of truth, comes, he will guide you into all the truth. He will not speak on his own; he will speak only what he hears, and he will tell you what is yet to come.*

This truth allows you to see your true self. This, in turn, allows you to take in God's truth and apply it to the very life He created you to live!! Ephesians 2:10 - *For we are God's handiwork, created in Christ Jesus to do good works, which God prepared in advance for us to do.* When you begin to live THE life He created you to live, stress begins to disappear. You will no longer feel a need to compete or compare with others. You will love people differently. You will experience an inexpressible and glorious joy (1 Peter 1:9). Then, my friend, the set of your mind will have been transformed as Paul wrote in Romans 12:2 - *Do not conform to the pattern of this world but be transformed by the renewing of your mind. Then you will be able to test and approve what God's will is—his good, pleasing, and perfect will.*

Then you will know God's perfect will for your life!!! How awesome is that!!! Talk about walking in confidence!

Chapter 4
Vision Casting

I touched on this earlier when describing some of the characteristics that Jesus employed while building His team. Vision casting is the thing that causes people to buy into paying the price required for where a person wants to go or for attaining the level of success a person wants. Jesus was constantly casting vision to help His followers keep their eyes fixed on where they were going or what they would attain. In the case of Jesus, His message centered around a life of eternity.
There is another biblical figure that we can learn great leadership qualities from Nehemiah. You should grab a bible, or get on a Bible app and read through Nehemiah. He exhibits several vital traits for success; obedience, humility, strength, courage, decisiveness, and yes, vision. Let's examine how Nehemiah caught and cast vision.

Nehemiah is the cup-bearer to king Artaxerxes. Meaning, he drank the wine before the king to ensure it was not poisoned. Yikes! He gets word that his homeland, Jerusalem, is in ruins. He begins to fast, pray, and ask God for wisdom on what he should do. God had given him a vision of what He wanted Nehemiah to do. We know this because when Nehemiah was before the king, he was sad.

This was punishable by death. The king asks Nehemiah what was wrong. Nehemiah tells the king what is bothering him. The king then asks.. *"what is it you want?"* Nehemiah quickly prays in the moment and asks the king. This was a big ask!! This was not something Nehemiah was trying to figure out in the moment. He had already been dreaming and planning what is needed to accomplish the task that God put on his heart. Surely, God was giving him the wisdom he needed before the king.

Artaxerxes gives Nehemiah <u>everything</u> he requested, and off to Jerusalem, he goes. Once Nehemiah arrives in Jerusalem, the real work begins. He scouts out the situation on his own (Nehemiah 2:11-16) as he formulates a plan. Then, he begins casting a vision to the people of Jerusalem.

Neh. 2:17-18 - *Then I said to them, "You see the trouble we are in: Jerusalem lies in ruins, and its gates have been burned with fire. Come, let us rebuild the wall of Jerusalem, and we will no longer be in disgrace." [18] I also told them about the gracious hand of my God on me and what the king had said to me. They replied, "Let us start rebuilding." So they began this good work.*

Nehemiah shared what God had done to even allow the work to begin. This included the favor of the king, all of the needed supplies along the way, soldiers to protect them while they traveled. Literally, everything they needed was supplied. As Nehemiah shared this, the confidence of the people grew. They began to 'catch' the vision. As they did, their own belief grew. Once the wall was halfway completed, more opposition came. The people were tired. Their "strength was giving out." There was so much rubble, and it was hard to work. Their enemies were threatening to attack them.

Neh. 4:6-12 - *So we rebuilt the wall till all of it reached half its height, for the people worked with all their heart.[7] But when Sanballat, Tobiah, the Arabs, the Ammonites and the people of Ashdod heard that the repairs to Jerusalem's walls had gone ahead and that the gaps were being closed, they were very angry. [8] They all plotted together to come and fight against Jerusalem and stir up trouble against it. [9] But we prayed to our God and posted a guard day and night to meet this threat.[10] Meanwhile, the people in Judah said, "The strength of the laborers is giving out, and there is so much rubble that we cannot rebuild the wall."[11] Also, our enemies said, "Before they know it or see us, we will be right there among them and will kill them and put an end to the work."[12] Then the Jews who lived near them came and told us ten times over, "Wherever you turn, they will attack us."*

Then, Nehemiah reading the situation accurately, makes a plan for how to work through the challenges and then the re-casts vision. He reminds them of what God had done to make them successful. Neh. 4:14 - *After I looked things over, I stood up and said to the nobles, the officials and the rest of the people, "Don't be afraid of them. Remember the Lord, who is great and awesome, and fight for your families, your sons and your daughters, your wives, and your homes."*

As you build your business, you will face challenges. People will tire. Opposition will come against you. You will gain momentum and lose it. There will be victories and defeats. You will reach goals and fail to reach them. Through it all, vision will be the driving force. Knowing exactly where you are going and helping others get to where they want to be in life is what vision is all about. You must be able to see the path before you can walk the path. It begins with seeing the path in your mind's eye. Vision, not sight. Vision is something different than sight. For the most part, sight is seeing that which already is. Vision sees beyond what is, to what is yet to be. It is combined with faith. And, as believers, *we are called to live by faith, not by sight - 2 Cor. 5:7*

Also, that vision is not something that is taught, it is caught. Clearly communicating vision draws the right people to it. Not everyone will buy in as they are called to something different. But, if you are clear on where you are going, your vision is compelling and clearly communicated, it will impact the people who find value for their own lives in pursuing your vision.

When God, the Father, called Abraham (Abram, at the time he was called), to leave his home. To leave everything he had known. To leave his comfort zone and go somewhere that God would show him. Abram was willing to go. When he left, though, he was not sure where he would end up. Why did he leave? Let's look.....

Gen. 12:1-3 - *The LORD had said to Abram, "Go from your country, your people and your father's household to the land I will show you.² "I will make you into a great nation, and I will bless you; I will make your name great, and you will be a blessing.³ I will bless those who bless you and whoever curses you I will curse and all peoples on earth will be blessed through you."*

Do you see it? God casting vision! Honestly, if God showed up in my room tonight and asked me to move somewhere else, told me he would bless me, my family, and everything I did, I would be pretty excited to go. The point here is that God cast a vision to inspire Abram to go. Now, Jesus, being God in the flesh, was involved as well. As we covered in chapter 2, Jesus also cast vision to His followers. While technology, cultures, and various other things have changed, human nature has not. Humans desire to be part of something bigger than themselves. This is why vision is so important. People can see beyond where they are currently. This hope of a greater reality motivates them to attempt greater things. Things are bigger than themselves. God knew it back in Abram's day. Jesus knew it in His day. Leaders of today know it presently.

If you are not a great vision caster or have simply never felt like you had a vision to communicate, there are some things you can do to improve. First, watch and listen to those that have great success in your chosen field. Those that have a strong following do so for a reason. They have developed the skill of casting vision. And, yes, it is a skill. Therefore, it can be learned. As you watch and listen, pay attention to the words they use. They will create word pictures for people. Meaning, they will say things that allow people to see themselves in a greater reality. They inspire others to be greater than they might otherwise believe. Making the picture clear by providing details and creating a path for people to mentally walk from where they are to where they want to be. It is not enough for you to be able to see your vision; you must help put others there in their own imagination. Your words – the pictures you paint with your words – are the key to getting others to buy in and follow you.

Secondly, if you don't believe that you have a compelling vision, then you must work on your own belief in what you are currently pursuing. Are you fully committed to success? Fully? If you are not, don't expect others to follow. If you are, then ask yourself whether you are thinking big enough? Are self-limiting beliefs impacting your thinking? Your imagination? If these things plague your thinking, read more books. Get around people that out-think you. This will help you grow your own thinking. As you get around bigger thinking more often, your own thinking will grow. Over time it will become normal for you. Then, the magic occurs. You will believe that you belong at a higher level of success because....that is what is normal!! Even for you.

As you step into greater success, you will naturally talk bigger. Meaning, you will create bigger word pictures as you speak to others. This will inspire others to greater activity. And there you are... casting vision! As you have greater success, you will continue to help others overcome their challenges. Walking along with them to be there when they experience discouragement. Many times, as a leader, you will have already walked where your team members are walking. Because we have been there, we can empathize with them. I heard a great quote years ago – "Mountaintops inspire leaders, valleys mature them." If you desire to be a great leader, you must be willing to "through" valleys. That is where your maturity is formed.

Chapter 5
Overcoming Disappointment

Speaking of valleys, know that we all go through them. Everyone! Too many believe that difficult times are a sign that a certain decision to grow in your life, is somehow wrong. Thinking like that is evidence of a weak mindset. If this is you, it is a sure sign that you need to grow your mental toughness. Your intestinal fortitude. Here is the reality: success is hard! As you pursue anything worthwhile, the journey to your destination will always include disappointment. It is a toll you pay along the highway to success. That being the case, it is best to mentally prepare before you begin. Simply being aware that disappointment will come, will allow you to appreciate it when it comes. Why? There are great lessons when things don't go as we expected them to.

Each time a person takes on a new endeavor, regardless of what it might be, the same process occurs. In this text, we are speaking specifically about Network Marketing. However, this applies to all endeavors. Here's out it goes…. We get a vision for a better life, situation, relationship, whatever. Then, our imagination goes to work on it. These imaginings are positive and negative. When a person gives into the negative imaginings (thoughts), fear sets in. Thoughts of quitting.

"Realistic" results tell us not to dream or think too big. However, when we give into and follow the positive imaginings, we see a picture of success. The challenge that often occurs is that our "imagined expectations" are not based in reality. We set very lofty goals without a real, solid plan to get us there. When 'reality' does not meet our imagined expectations, disappointment sets in. You see, plans are great. Reality is greater!

Perhaps the clearest example of this is the time in which we currently live. 2020 has brought one challenge after another for basically all of us. Those who were mentally prepared would farewell. Those that weren't have struggled. Many business owners across the U.S. have had to deal with circumstances no one saw coming. Many have closed doors for good. As the year began, as people normally do, goals were set. Plans were made. Expectations were high. Then, reality set in with the introduction of Covid-19, followed by worldwide lockdowns. This brought on a financial crisis – some are yet to be seen. Then, in the US, protests, and riots broke out. Fear, anger, rage, uncertainty, among other emotions, have caused many to re-evaluate their plans and goals. Again, plans are great. Reality is greater.

James, the half-brother of Jesus, states it this way: *Now listen, you who say, "Today or tomorrow we will go to this or that city, spend a year there, carry on business and make money."* ¹⁴ *Why, you do not even know what will happen tomorrow. What is your life? You are a mist that appears for a little while and then vanishes.* ¹⁵ *Instead, you ought to say, "If it is the Lord's will, we will live and do this or that."* James 4:13-15

With that said, how then should we go about making plans? Setting goals? Is it wrong to do that? Of course, not. However, as mentioned earlier, we must be prepared for setbacks. Be ready for changing circumstances. You have probably heard the quote, "plans change, decisions don't." This is exactly what is required to overcome disappointment. So, as you set goals, know this; *In their hearts, humans plan their course, but the LORD establishes their steps.* Prov. 16:9
As a believer in Christ, I believe that God is omniscient. He knows all – from beginning to end, all at the same time. Therefore, God knows what is yet to come. Fortunately, prior to Jesus' ascent to heaven, He told His followers that He would send a "helper. The comforter, The Holy Spirit.

But when he, the Spirit of truth, comes, he will guide you into all the truth. He will not speak on his own; he will speak only what he hears, and he will tell you what is yet to come. John 16:13

This is important to grasp because you can get wisdom from the Holy Spirit (God living in you) when setting goals and making plans. We can make more firm plans when we seek God's will, examine our lives, desire to please God with our thoughts, words, and actions. When *we are led by the Spirit, we can keep in step with the Spirit* (Gal. 5:25). Now, this does not mean that we will not have setbacks or disappointments. It simply means that we can make plans that do not oppose or mock God. When disappointment comes, we must be ready to deal with it. We use the term – Champions adjust! Simply assess what is happening, and if a pivot is required, so be it. When a space ship is headed for a planet, or to the moon, the majority of the time it is off-course. Corrections are constantly being made. Assume the same in whatever endeavor you are pursuing.

In my opinion, the vast majority of 'disappointments' that come are good for us. You see, through tough times, we learn who we really are. We learn what our faith is truly made of. Do we really believe in what we are doing and where we are going? By walking through disappointment, we grow. We mature.

Remember, mountaintops inspire leaders, valleys mature them! It is only in the valley where we truly grow. Within a Network marketing company, having gone through tough times, we are able to look others in the eye and tell them with all conviction...I know where you are. I have been there. Let me tell you what God did through that time. He will do it for you! You have probably heard this laid out at a personal development event this way – "I know how you feel, I felt the same way, here's what I found." Referred to as "feel, felt, found." This truth is found in 2 Cor. 1

Praise be to the God and Father of our Lord Jesus Christ, the Father of compassion and the God of all comfort, 4 who comforts us in all our troubles, so that we can comfort those in any trouble with the comfort we ourselves receive from God. 2 Cor. 1:3,4

I often use this phrase in describing our journey through life... "we live life forward, understand it backwards." Many times, it can be difficult to see God's hand at work IN our trials. However, as we look back over our lives, it becomes easier to see how God orchestrates events for our benefit. *"And we know that in all things God works for the good of those who love him, who have been called according to his purpose."* Rom. 8:28. As we are able to see how all of the pieces fit together in our past, we can draw greater confidence that God will continue to do the very same things in our future. As this truth becomes our truth, we can face disappointment with confidence that God will take away. He will use it all for our good! Over time, we will actually welcome trials, disappointment, and struggle, because we become certain that we will be better because of them. We can change our perspective and look at setbacks differently.

Think of the term (or reality) of a "set-back" as a "set -(up for a come)- back"!! You see, when you begin to embrace disappointment, difficult times, etc., then you will grow through them. More importantly, you will go through them faster. They will not steal your energy, drive, passion, and vision. They will only strengthen you. After you have persevered through many challenges, your mindset and mental fortitude will grow so much, that many others will marvel at how stable you are. How confidently you move through struggles. This is why your foundation in Christ is so vital. You can see trials from God's perspective, which is always good. As you live life this way consistently, more will be willing to follow you because they will see a strength in you that is admirable. They will be attracted to it. To you! So, be prepared for the stop-lights, tolls, and detours along the way to your destination. You will navigate them more effectively.

Another indispensable benefit to walking through trials and disappointment is a perfected faith.

Consider it pure joy, my brothers and sisters, whenever you face trials of many kinds because you know that the testing of your faith produces perseverance. Let perseverance finish its work so that you may be mature and complete, not lacking anything.
James 1:2-4

What I am about to cover is vitally important to understand. Be sure that you have a few minutes of focused time as you read what follows. How does one learn to consider trials "pure joy"? This is an easy verse to read, but difficult to live out. I remember when I would encounter trials early in my life, my mind would drift to all kinds of imagined possibilities. Many people imagine the worst possible outcome, which then leads to anxiety. Not having experience on my side, I would sometimes be paralyzed by the fear of my imagination. You have heard it many times, right? FEAR = False Evidence Appearing Real. When trials come, fear can set in. Or, frustration, or anger, or discouragement, or despair, or... on and on. You have probably been there. We get to a point where we cry out, "why is this happening!". The trials can shake us.

Over time, however, when we have walked through some trials correctly, this can change. Correctly, meaning asking God for help, patience, wisdom, etc. We see God move and realize that through the trial, we can actually grow. When this happens just once, it can build our confidence. This is typically not a fast process. We want what we want! Many times, what we "want" is for the trial – more accurately, the pain of the trial – to simply go away. I am guessing you are nodding your head about now. If we, as followers of Christ, could truly grasp the truth of this passage early on, we would grow even faster.

You see, at 57 years old now, I have enough experience in walking through many, many trials, that I truly believe that trials are good! I do consider it pure joy when they come. Don't get me wrong, I don't like the trials. I want everything to work just like I want it to, in my time frame. Just like you. However, those trials, challenges, heartbreak, relational challenges, etc., come for a specific reason. They "test our faith" (verse 3 above). It is not only important; it is necessary. That testing of our faith produces perseverance. We learn what we actually believe only in the trials. We can say we have faith all day long. We can recite our 'belief' to others easily when all is going great. Heck, that does not require much faith. It is in the struggle that our real faith is borne out. It is only then when we decide to keep moving or give up. I watch this in Network Marketing day after day after day.

When people run into difficult times, they tend to shut down. It goes back to that mental fortitude that has not yet been developed. When they shut down, they realize way down deep inside, that they were not as committed as they had professed. When that happens, our core belief is impacted. We know that we are not who we said we were because our actions proved it out.

What good is it, my brothers and sisters, if someone claims to have faith but has no deeds? Can such faith save them? 15 Suppose a brother or a sister is without clothes and daily food. 16 If one of you says to them, "Go in peace; keep warm and well fed," but does nothing about their physical needs, what good is it? 17 In the same way, faith by itself, if it is not accompanied by action, is dead. But someone will say, "You have faith; I have deeds." Show me your faith without deeds, and I will show you my faith by my deeds.
James 2:14-18

James is making his point concerning his faith in God. That faith, if it is real, will be borne out in deeds (action). The truth of this applies to every one of us in our faith walk in following Christ. It equally plays out in our daily and business life. As an example, if I am married to someone and tell them daily that I love them, yet at the same time, I am cheating on them, my actions prove that my words are false. Over time, my actions will speak louder than my words. Years ago, a friend said it this way…. "Who you are speaks so loudly that what you say, I cannot hear!"

Ok, how does all of this relate to overcoming disappointment, and why are trials joyful?

The essence of this book is to give foundational truth that allowed Jesus to spend three years building a movement that continues to grow today. These truths are so deep that they transcend time, fads, culture, etc. The truth in James 1:2-8 is more profound than most understand. Trials teach perseverance. Persevering builds our belief that we deserve what we are pursuing (our goal). The belief that you/we 'deserve' success is vital as it goes back to our self-limiting beliefs. *For as he thinketh in his heart, so is he.* Prov. 23:7. When you believe that you deserve more success, you will find it! Conversely, if you don't believe it, you will stay right where you are!

As you move through the passage to verse 4, perseverance ends by making us mature. Not lacking anything. It literally perfects our faith. As we mature, we grow. Because we have walked through trials, we can look back and see the growth we have had. We then realize that the result of the trial was good because we are better for it. The more this happens, the more we realize that trials are actually good. Again, when this becomes 'our' truth, we can consider trials pure joy because we are about to get better! Get 'perfected'! When this happens, our 'cry' of "why is this happening?" Changes. Instead of crying out in frustration, fear, anger, etc. We ask it in a different way. With maturity, Lord, why is this happening? Meaning, God, help me understand the purpose of this trial. What do I need to learn from it?

Now, there is more to this passage. Many times, when we are going through trials, we are asking for help. Verse 5 tells us that if we lack wisdom, we can ask God for it. He gives it 'generously to all without finding fault.'

If any of you lacks wisdom, you should ask God, who gives generously to all without finding fault, and it will be given to you. But when you ask, you must believe and not doubt, because the one who doubts is like a wave of the sea, blown and tossed by the wind. That person should not expect to receive anything from the Lord. Such a person is double-minded and unstable in all they do. James 5-8

God literally helps us when we are going through trials/challenges. Now, listen. When you ask for help….. wait for it! *Be still and know that I am God.* Ps. 46:10. Too many of us want to run ahead and do what we think we need to do to fix the problem. James calls this 'double-minded.' You ask God for help and then do your own thing. He says that this person 'should not expect to receive anything from the Lord'. Yikes! God doesn't just want to end your trial; he wants to perfect you in the process. Trials come for a reason, friend. Accept them for your good. Allow the struggle to grow you, not stop you. Get better, not bitter. There will be no end to future trials, struggles, challenges, disappointments, etc. At least, not this side of Heaven. Take God at His word.

Chapter 6
Love Wins!

Well, we have covered some territory. We have learned the importance of building your life and your business on a solid foundation. We reviewed the principles Jesus used to build His network and why a proper mindset is not only necessary, but possible. Hopefully, 'caught' how and why to cast vision and how to overcome discouragement. All of these points are necessary to succeed in life and, more specifically, in Network Marketing. However, while it is important to grow your mindset and skill-set, without the last ingredient, it will all be fleeting. If you want to build large, strong, tight teams, you must Love your people! Without love, well, let's see what the apostle Paul said about it:

If I speak in the tongues of men or of angels but do not have love, I am only a resounding gong or a clanging cymbal. If I have the gift of prophecy and can fathom all mysteries and all knowledge, and if I have a faith that can move mountains, but does not have love, I am nothing. If I give all I possess to the poor and give over my body to hardship that I may boast, but do not have love, I gain nothing. 1 Cor. 12:1-3

When you are building a team, the adage is true, and people don't care how much you know until they know how much you care! You cannot escape it. Loving others is what makes it all work. Not just in our industry but in our world, as well. When we come from a place of love for others, we can walk through storms together. When difficult times come, our care for others will be the glue that binds us. When I need to have difficult conversations with one of my team members, I lead with love, and they know it. Over time, my love and concern for them have been proven over weeks, months, or years. They know that they can trust me. Prov. 27:6 says *Wounds from a friend can be trusted.* Because my team members know I have their best interest in mind, they know that when I provide hard information, it is for their benefit. If I try to correct without love, it is just criticism.

Paul then defines what love actually is...

Love is patient, love is kind. It does not envy, it does not boast, it is not proud. It does not dishonor others, it is not self-seeking, it is not easily angered, it keeps no record of wrongs. Love does not delight in evil but rejoices with the truth. It always protects, always trusts, always hopes, always perseveres. Love never fails. 1 Cor. 12:4-8

As you read what love is, I hope you recognize that each attribute is a choice. You choose to be patient with people. And, in our world, patience is precious. You will learn that you must be patient with people as we are all works in process. The personal growth process does not happen quickly. Many will tell you all about what they are about to do and then don't. Great intentions, without great actions to back it up. Watching people, we care about struggle because of habits, wrong thinking, negative attitudes, and a poor self-image hurts. You must be patient with others, just as your leaders have been and are patient with you.

Being kind is self-explanatory. Again, though, you choose to be kind. In all areas of life, if you don't treat others – all others – with kindness, you must resolve to change this. What you are dealing with is Pride. And as Paul continues, that is a choice. Don't envy, boast, and do not act in pride! Think about it; much of the list Paul outlines has to do with humility. As he writes in Philippians 2:3,4:

Do nothing out of selfish ambition or vain conceit. Rather, in humility value others above yourselves, not looking to your own interests but each of you to the interests of the others.

As mentioned in the introduction, this happens to be my life verse. When I fully understood the Network Marketing business, I am involved with, and I realized that I could now be paid for living out that verse. Talk about liberating! Loving others means putting their interests ahead of yours. The bigger your organization grows, the more you will realize that your rights move further down the priority list. This is because there are more and more people that you are putting ahead of yourself. If you operate from an attitude of love and care, this is an easier thing to do.

If you operate from a place of pride, loving others will not be easy. Those around will be offended sooner or later by that pride – and leave. Remember, *God opposes the proud but gives grace to the humble.* James 4:6. Also, recall that pride is what got Satan kicked out of heaven! So, if you want God to bless your efforts, do what pleases Him. Love God, love people. *Act justly, love mercy, and walk humbly with your God.* Micah 6:8. Pride and humility cannot co-exist. Check your heart. When loving God is our priority, loving people follow. Operate for an audience of one. Please, God, surrender to His will, and then He becomes responsible for the outcome of your life.

Before leaving the "love" passage, I want to point out one more important, but little known truth. Forgiveness. 'Love keeps no record of wrongs.' There is much to say about forgiveness. I will touch on only a couple of truths. Jesus himself said:

For if you forgive other people when they sin against you, your heavenly Father will also forgive you. But if you do not forgive others their sins, your Father will not forgive your sins. Mat. 6:14,15

If you want your Heavenly Father to forgive you, you need to forgive others. Forgiving others when they have wronged, you requires humility and love. In an industry like ours, it is clear that we are in the people business. It can get messy. Keeping short accounts will keep much stress out of your life. Always trust in God, not people. *All have sinned and fall short of the glory of God.* Rom. 3:23. People will let you down. Why? Because we are human and we make mistakes. Too often, we judge others by their actions while judging ourselves by our intentions! We give ourselves way more grace than we extend to others. If you could treat your team members as your children, if you have them, and love them like you love your children, forgive them like your children, and hope for them like you hope for your children, you will love them into becoming who God created them to be. This is what love is all about. Love always protects, trusts, hopes perseveres. I pray that you grasp how powerful, loving others is.

Separately, when we don't forgive others, Satan is literally outwitting us.

Anyone you forgive, I also forgive. And what I have forgiven—if there was anything to forgive—I have forgiven in the sight of Christ for your sake, [11] in order that <u>Satan might not outwit us</u>. For we are not unaware of his schemes. 2 Cor. 2:10,11

There will be plenty of turmoil in the world. People issues, product issues to deal with, business setbacks, etc. We don't need to also be outwitted by Satan on top of it all. If we don't forgive, we will not hear clearly from the Lord. When you seek answers, they will be difficult to hear. God's word is clear. Unforgiveness gives Satan a foothold, which can become a stronghold – anger, bitterness, resentment, etc. When these negative emotions control your life, our enemy has you right where he wants you. *He is prowling around like a roaring lion looking for someone to devour.* 1 Peter 5:8. Think about how lions hunt. They try to isolate the weak. If Satan can get you bitter and resentful, it is easier to isolate you. Then, he devours! When you don't forgive, you become the prisoner. We are in the people business. The relationships are the key to greater success. Forgive others. Love everyone. Lead those who are ready to be led!

Lastly, you got started in business for a reason. You saw something 'more.' You had/have hopes of a better future. Without that hope, there would be no need for faith that you can attain what you hope for. As an example, I am under 6 ft. and 57 years old. I have no 'hope' of playing professional basketball. Therefore, no 'faith' is required to achieve what I don't hope for. Since I don't have faith, no action is required to prove my faith. Hope is the catalyst. In a business like ours, hope becomes the driver, and literally, anyone can be successful in our industry. Your age doesn't matter, your background, educational level, ethnicity, gender, race, etc., none of it matters. If you want more success, you can have it in our industry. It is the great equalizer. So, yes, get your hopes up, and then protect that hope. Nurture it. Get around others that support where you want to go. Once you have hope, then, faith is required, and action follows. Paul shares this truth:

···because we have heard of your faith in Christ Jesus and of the love you have for all God's people— 5 the faith and love that spring

from the hope stored up for you in heaven,
Col. 1:4,5

You see, faith and love spring from hope. The hope comes first. When we hope for a better future, action is also required, as we touched on in Overcoming Disappointment. However, your action will be in direct correlation with the faith you have in attaining the hope you have. When your faith in succeeding wains, your activity will follow and vice versa. As your faith grows, so will your activity. When your activity increases, your results will increase. Increased results, in turn, will grow your faith as you draw nearer to what you hope for. Through the process, you will grow and mature. You will no longer operate from emotion, as a child does. But you will have greater resolve. The ups and downs won't sway you. Paul stated this way:

When I was a child, I talked like a child, I thought like a child, I reasoned like a child. When I became a man {mature}, I put the ways of childhood behind me. [12] *For now, we see only a reflection as in a mirror; then we shall see face to face. Now I know in part; then I shall know fully, even as I am fully known. And now these three remain: faith, hope, and love. But the greatest of these is love.* 1 Cor. 13:11-13

Love wins!

Conclusion

You and I were 'created' in the image of God, our 'creator.' Since we were 'created' by a 'creative' God, in His image, that means that we, too, are 'creative.' We are here to create. What the mind of man can conceive and believe, it can achieve! You, Christ-follower, *have the mind of Christ. 2 Cor. 2:16.* Ask the God that created you for wisdom on how to proceed and wait for His answer. You are created as a Masterpiece in God's eyes. Know that you were 'created' for way more than you know! You have found an industry that rewards a life lived to glorify our God, through Jesus Christ, our savior. Do that with everything you have now. What you lack, continue to improve. Keep Christ at the center of your life. *Take delight in the LORD, and he will give you the desires of your heart. Ps. 37:4.* God knows your desires. When you prioritize God's purposes, your desires change. That is why He gives you the desires of your heart. Because they align with His will and purpose for creating you! Now, as God told Noah, after the flood.... *As for you, be fruitful and increase in number; multiply on the earth and increase upon it. Gen. 9:7.* LOL.

Tere Kampe

This is a slightly different context, but still, it is the goal of what we are to do, 5000 years later.

May God, the creator of the universe, who knows all things from beginning to end, all at the same time, bless you mightily. May He bless the work of your hands as you glorify Him.

Amen!

About The Author

Tere has been around the Network Marketing industry for 48 years. During that time, roughly 20 of those years were spent trying to build a successful business. Many of those years did not look like success. After realizing that his self-limiting beliefs were a big part of the problem, He turned to God for answers. This allowed Tere to finally understand how to succeed at a higher level in life. He worked as a sales rep for 17 years in the High purity chemical arena while trying to build his Networking business. He is married to his wife, Mary, now for 27 years. Has three daughters and two grandchildren.

Prior to being introduced to his current company, Tere volunteered at his church as an elder and led the Men's Ministry for several years. After achieving the top rank in his current company, God then called him to Pastor a new campus for the church he was attending, in 2016. Tere pastored there for three years before leaving silicon valley for Las Vegas, where he currently resides. Tere is involved in corporate leadership and participates in prayer groups with a select group of men and women who seek God's direction and vision for his current company. He also preaches at the non-denominational worship services that occur at the company's major events throughout the year. He is a million-dollar earner and a member of the President's Advisory Council with his current company. Additionally, he is one of the elite personal and leadership development trainers for the company.

Tere is actively involved in mentoring and developing leaders all over the world. His passion is helping people become all God, creating them to be. Walking others through their belief issues and leadership, lids fuels him.

Made in the USA
Las Vegas, NV
17 November 2020